W9-CSS-114

The Chili & Tomato Cookbook

Jonathan Freestone

The American Pantry Collection ™

Published by:
Apricot Press
Box 1611
American Fork, Utah
84003

books@apricotpress.com
www.apricotpress.com

ISBN 1-885027-20-6

Designed by David Mecham
Printed in the United States of America

Forward

Chilies and Tomatoes: two of my favorite foods. I hope you relish them like I do. Some sumptuous recipes follow, which I am confident will enhance your enjoyment of these wonderful red and green delicacies. Bon Apetit!

Jonathan Freestone

Recipes

Tangy Tomato Pancakes

2 cups stewed tomatoes with liquid
40 single saltine soda crackers, crushed
salt to taste
2 tbsp. butter

Instructions:

Blend all ingredients in bowl. Shape into 4 to 6-inch pancakes and fry in a small amount of butter (over medium heat about 2 minutes on each side). Makes about 12 (4-in.) pancakes.

Ensalada - Sized and shaped like a plum tomato. However, it tastes like it belongs in the beefsteak family

Tomato & Zucchini Pie

2 medium tomatoes, chopped
2 cups chopped zucchini
1/2 medium bell pepper, chopped
1 medium onion, chopped
1/3 cup grated parmesan cheese
3 large eggs, thoroughly beaten
1-1/2 cups Bisquick
salt and pepper to taste

Instructions:

Preheat oven to 400 degrees. Grease 10 inch pie plate. Place tomato, pepper, zucchini, onion and cheese in plate. In blender, whip remaining ingredients until smooth. Pour into pie plate and bake until firm (10 or 15 minutes). Serve as is or top with salsa and sour cream.

Tomato Scramble

Ingredients:

2 medium tomatoes, cubed
4 egg whites
4 egg yolks
2/3 cup evaporated milk
1 tbsp. flour
1/2 tsp. salt
1/2 tsp. pepper
1/2 lb. Cheddar cheese, grated
1/2 lb. Monterey Jack cheese, grated
1/4 tsp. cream of tartar

Instructions:

Separate egg yolks from whites. Beat egg whites until stiff; mix with other ingredients. Line well-buttered pan with grated Cheddar and Monterey Jack cheeses. Pour over cheeses in pan. Bake at 375 degrees for 20 minutes or until set.

Tomato Truths

-Today we find tomatoes everywhere, in salads, sauces, and gardens. It's hard to imagine that not all that long ago, they were thought to be poisonous. In the early 1500s, shortly after Hernando Cortez conquered Mexico, Conquistadores brought the tomato to Europe. Even though Native Americans enjoyed them, because it was a relative of the deadly nightshade family of plants, Europeans were highly suspicious. Tomatoes caught on in Spain first, but the Italians would not accept them widely for 200 more years. Imagine Italian cooking without tomatoes.

Yellow Pear - An heirloom variety beloved for its heavy clusters of pear-shaped, small tomatoes.

Colorado Egg Bake

3 large eggs
1-1/2 cups tomatoes, chopped
1/2 cup tomato sauce
1/4 cup chopped green chilies (or as many as you like)
2 tbsp. chopped onion
2 cloves garlic
1/2 tsp. ground cumin
4 whole cloves
1/4 tsp. dried thyme
4 tbsp. water
1/2 cup oil
4 corn tortillas
4 tbsp. refried beans
4 tbsp. diced ham
grated Cheddar cheese
salt and pepper to taste

Instructions:
In a blender, puree onion, garlic, cumin, cloves, thyme, and water.
Strain. Heat 2 tbsp. oil in a small saucepan, add the puree and stir
for one minute. Add tomato, chilies, tomato sauce and salt and
cook for 5 minutes. Set this mixture aside. Heat the remaining oil
in a skillet. Fry each tortilla for 30 seconds, turning if necessary.
Remove the tortillas and place on a plate. Pour off the oil, add eggs
and fry or scramble until set.

Place a tortilla on a plate. Spread half of the beans on a tortilla.
Place half the eggs on beans. Cover with the other tortilla, spoon
the tomato salsa on top and garnish with ham and cheese. Repeat
to make 2 servings.

Tomato & Cheese Breakfast Casserole

Ingredients:

6 large eggs, lightly beaten
1/2 cup Swiss cheese, grated
1/2 cup Cheddar cheese, grated
2 medium tomatoes, chopped
3 cups sourdough croutons
2 cups milk
1/2 tsp. Worcestershire sauce
1 tsp. dry mustard
2 cups baked ham, cubed
2 tbsp. fresh parsley
1/2 tsp. salt
1/2 tsp. pepper

Instructions:

Place croutons in bottom of greased casserole dish. Cover croutons
with cheeses. Combine other ingredients (except parsley) in bowl
and mix thoroughly. Pour mixture over cheese and croutons.
Sprinkle parsley on top. Bake at 350 degrees until firm. (50 to 60
minutes).

Salads

Downtown Taco Salad

Ingredients:

1 lb. ground beef
1 taco seasoning packet
1 can garbanzo beans, drained
1 can kidney beans, drained
3 medium tomatoes, diced
1 avocado, peeled, pitted, and diced
2-1/2 cups Cheddar cheese, grated
1 onion , diced
1 head of lettuce, chopped
4 to 6 oz. of tortilla chips, broken into pieces
salt and pepper to taste
salsa and sour cream for garnish

Instructions :

In sauce pan, brown the ground beef. Season with salt and pepper and taco seasoning packet, following directions on package. Set this browned meat aside and allow to cool slightly while you make the rest of the salad. Mix together the lettuce, garbanzo, and kidney beans, cheese, avocado, tomatoes, and onions. Add tortilla chips and meat last, toss, and serve. Top with sour cream and salsa if desired. Makes 4 servings.

Avocado Stuffed Tomatoes

Ingredients:

4 medium tomatoes
1 large, ripe avocado
2 tsp. lemon juice
1/2 tsp. chili powder
1/2 cup alfalfa sprouts
2 tbsp. chopped celery
1/2 green bell pepper, chopped
1 tsp. chopped parsley
1/2 tsp. coriander
salt to taste

Instructions:

Cut tops off tomatoes & scoop out insides. Mash avocado & mix in the other ingredients. Stuff mixture into the tomato shells. Enjoy! Goes well with main dish or as appetizer.
Serves 4.

Poblano - Know as an Ancho pepper when dried. Mild to medium flavor. Commonly used in Rellenos when available.

El Paso Marinated Tomatoes

Ingredients:

4 medium tomatoes, thinly sliced
3 tbsp. balsamic vinegar
1/4 cup olive oil
1/4 cup canola oil
1 tsp. Worcestershire sauce
3/4 tsp. salt
1/2 tsp. black pepper
1 tbsp. sugar
2 garlic cloves, minced
2 tsp. basil, chopped
1/4 tsp. thyme

Instructions:

Place sliced tomatoes in bowl. Blend all other ingredients in a separate bowl. Pour the marinade over the tomatoes. Cover & refrigerate for at least 1 hour before serving.

Peppers & Pasta Salad

4 3-oz. skinless chicken breasts
1/4 tbsp. chili powder
1 tsp. ground cumin
1 tsp. vegetable oil
1/2 cup water
1/2 tsp. chicken bouillon granules
1 small ripe avocado, chopped
1 cup fresh cilantro, chopped
3 tbsp. of fresh lime juice
1/4 cup green onions, chopped
1 large jalapeno pepper, chopped
1 clove of garlic
1/4 cup black olives, sliced
1 cup chopped tomatoes
1/2 cup shredded zucchini
6 oz. uncooked fettuccine

Sprinkle chicken with cumin and chili powder. Heat oil in a medium skillet; add chicken and cook over medium heat for 3 to 4 minutes on each side. Add water and bouillon granules; reduce heat and simmer for 15 minutes or until chicken is done. Remove chicken from broth (save broth in skillet.) Cover and chill chicken. Bring broth to a boil and cook until reduced to 1/4 cup. Remove from heat and cool. Pour broth, avocado, cilantro, lime juice, garlic, onions, and peppers into food processor. Process until smooth. Cook fettuccine according to package directions. Drain and rinse under cold water. Place in center of a serving platter. Arrange zucchini around fettuccine-avocado mixture. Cut chilled chicken into 1/4 inch strips and arrange over fettuccini. Sprinkle with chopped cilantro.
Makes 4 servings.

Spinach & Pepper Salad

Ingredients:

1 red bell pepper cut into 1/4 inch strips
4 cups spinach leaves, rinsed
1 15-oz. can black beans, rinsed and drained
1/2 cup thin sliced onion, rings
1 cup sliced mushroom
1/4 cup canadian bacon, strips
1/2 cup picante sauce
1/4 cup Italian dressing
1/4 tsp. ground cumin
4 hard-boiled eggs, cut into wedges or slices

Instructions:

Combine vegetables, beans, and bacon in large bowl. Combine picante sauce, dressing, and cumin in separate bowl; mix well. Pour picante sauce mixture over vegetables. Toss lightly to coat with dressing. Chill. Toss again and garnish with eggs. If you like things hotter, serve with additional picante sauce. Serves 4.

Holy Frijole Black Bean Salad

Ingredients:

- 1 large tomato, skinned, chopped
- 1/4 cup chopped red bell pepper
- 1/4 cup chopped orange bell pepper
- 1/4 cup chopped green bell pepper
- 1 can black beans with jalapeno peppers, drained and washed
- 1 large green onion, chopped
- 1/2 tsp. sweet pickle relish
- 1/2 tsp. chopped garlic
- 1 tsp. vinegar
- 1 tbsp. lime
- 1/4 tsp. cumin
- salt and pepper to taste

Instructions:

Combine all ingredients in large bowl Blend and refrigerate for two hours. Enjoy.   Makes 4 servings.

Tomato Stuffed Zuchinni

Ingredients:

36 fresh cherry tomatoes
1-1/2 lbs. zucchini, peeled and shredded
1/4 cup raisins, chopped
1/4 tsp. salt
1/2 tsp. pepper
1-1/2 tbsp. pine nuts
1 tbsp. white wine vinegar

Instructions:

Trim a small slice off the top of each tomato, remove seeds, drain, and place side down, on paper towels. In a separate skillet, sauté zucchini, raisins, salt and pepper until nearly all liquid evaporates. Add vinegar. Spread mixture onto a plate and chill. Just prior to serving, stir in nuts, and spoon into tomatoes. Keep refrigerated until ready to serve. Makes 36 appetizers.

Big Thai - Hybrid variety with a rich pepper
flavor... once you get past the warmth.
Used widely in red pepper flakes.

Shining the Light on Tomatoes

-Recent studies have shown that people, especially men, who consume large amounts of tomatoes have lower cancer rates. Colon cancer rates are especially reduced. The chemical in tomatoes that researchers believe may help the body fight cancer is lycopene. Tomatoes are also rich in vitamins A and C.

-Today, there are more than 4,000 varieties of tomatoes grown in the world, from yellow pear tomatoes, to acidic beefsteaks.

-If we don't include the huge amount of tomatoes grown in backyard gardens, over 9 million tons of tomatoes are grown in the United States alone. Worldwide, the amount is nearly 10 times that.

San Antonio Macaroni Salad

Ingredients:

1 cup elbow or corkscrew pasta
salted water
2 medium carrots, shredded
3 green onions, thinly chopped
2 green or red peppers, chopped
1 jalapeno pepper seeded, deveined, chopped
1 cup sour cream
1/2 cup mayonnaise
1 tsp. white wine vinegar
salt and pepper to taste

Instructions:

Cook pasta in boiling salted water until tender (usually about seven minutes depending on altitude). Drain and let cool. Combine carrots, onions, and peppers in bowl. In another bowl mix mayonnaise, sour cream, and white vinegar. Pour mixture onto vegetables and mix well. Chill and enjoy.

Soups, Chili, and Chowders

Inca Chili & Potato Soup

Ingredients:

2 4-oz. cans chopped, green chilies
1 large onion, diced
1 tbsp. butter
2 10.75-oz. cans condensed cream of potato soup
21.5 oz. half and half
4 oz. monterey jack cheese

Instructions :

Sauté onions until tender. Place butter and sautéed onions into pot or Dutch oven. Add green chilies, soups, and half and half. Heat, but do not boil. Cube cheese into 1/2 inch pieces and place in the bottom of soup bowls. Pour soup into bowls and serve. Serves 4.

Christmas Grape - Mini-tomato variety prized for its sweet, rich flavor. Continues to grow fruit until the fall frost.

Tomato & Bean Soup

Ingredients:

1-1/2 cups navy beans
3 qts. water
1 qt. tomatoes
2 diced carrots
1/2 medium bell pepper-diced
1/3 cup rice
1 1/2 cups diced celery
1 small garlic bulb
1/3 cup diced onion
1 to 2 beef bouillon cubes
1/4 tsp. salt
1 lb. hamburger
1/3 cup green pepper
1 potato, cubed

Instructions:

Wash beans. Add water, boil for 3 minutes. Remove from heat and let soak for 1 hour. Simmer for 1/2 hour. Add tomatoes, peppers, potatoes, celery, carrots, rice, onions, salt, pepper, and bouillon. Bring to boil. Brown hamburger and add to soup. Simmer, covered for 1 hour until beans are tender.

Bacon & Beef Chili

Ingredients:

2 lbs. lean bacon
3 medium onions
1 lb. mushrooms
4 lbs. ground beef
4 16-oz. cans kidney beans with juice
3 16-oz. cans tomatoes with juice
1 tsp. sugar
1 tsp. cumin
1-1/2 tbsp. chili powder
*1/4 cup dried, hot chili's
salt and pepper to taste

*This assumes a fairly high tolerance for hot. Use more or less according to taste.

Instructions:

Cut bacon into 1/2 inch pieces; fry. Dice onion; sauté until transparent; then set aside. Fry ground beef; add bacon, onion, beans, chili and tomatoes. Stir on medium/high heat until heated through, then add seasonings. Lower heat to simmer and cook for 3 hours.

Tomato & Black Bean Soup

Ingredients:

28 oz. whole tomatoes, cut into 1-inch chunks
1 bell pepper, chopped
1 lb. black beans; dried
1 large onion (about 1 cup), chopped
4 garlic cloves, finely chopped
2 tbsp. vegetable oil
2 cups smoked ham or turkey ham, cooked and cubed
6 cups chicken broth
2 tbsp. red chilies, ground
2 tbsp. fresh cilantro, snipped
1 tbsp. oregano leaves, dried
2 tsp. ground cumin
1 chipotle chile (canned in Adobo sauce)

Instructions:

Cook onion and garlic in oil in 4 quart pot or Dutch oven, stirring all the while, until onion is tender. Stir in remaining ingredients and heat to a boil. Boil for 2 minutes; reduce heat. Cover and simmer until beans are tender, about 2 1/2 hours. Optional: Blend in food processor until smooth. Serve with diced bell pepper sprinkled on top and a dab of sour cream. Enjoy! Makes 8 to 10 servings.

Pondering Peppers

-The chemical in peppers that causes them to be hot is called capsaicin. Most of this capsaicin is stored on the ribs (What are the ribs? Open one up and see!) inside the chili pepper. As most peppers mature, the amount of the chemical increases.

-Use extreme caution when handling very hot peppers. Water will not bring relief if you should inadvertently rub a finger to your eye or nose. Capsaicin is readily transferred from fingers to eyes, even contact lenses during handling. This can cause extreme discomfort. Whenever handling extremely hot peppers, wear disposable gloves.

Caribbean Red - Super-hot habanero variety that packs twice the punch of the standard orange habanero (200 times hotter than a jalapeño).

Rio Grande Chili

Ingredients:

3 medium-sized tomatoes, diced
4 lbs. ground chuck or lean hamburger
1 large, yellow onion, chopped
2 cloves garlic, chopped
1 tsp. ground oregano
1 tsp. cumin seed
6 tsp. chili powder
1-1/2 cups canned whole tomatoes
2 to 6 generous dashes hot sauce
salt and pepper to taste
2 cups hot water

Instructions:

Place uncooked meat in skillet with onions and garlic. Saute until meat is light-colored, then add all other ingredients. Bring to a boil, then reduce heat, cover and simmer for about an hour. Skim off the fat during the cooking. Serves 10-12.

Chicken & Tomato Soup

Ingredients:

3 roma tomatoes, diced
2 chicken breast, halves
2 qts. chicken stock
1 large red onion, chopped
3 corn tortillas, fried and broken
1/2 bunch cilantro
8 oz. ancho chile paste
6 oz. ranchero cheese, shredded
2 corn tortillas, fried crisp
salt and pepper to taste

Instructions :

Boil chicken breasts in 2-1/2 quarts water until thoroughly cooked. Remove chicken from bone in small pieces. In large skillet or Dutch oven, bring 1 quart chicken broth and chopped onion to a boil. In a blender, blend the remaining chicken broth and 3 fried tortillas until slightly thickened. Pour mixture into heated broth. Add tomatoes, cilantro, chile paste, and chicken. Season to taste with salt and pepper. Bring to boil again. Serve in bowls garnished with cheese and tortilla strips. Makes 8 servings.

Peppers & Mushroom Chili

Ingredients:

> 1 lb. ground beef
> 1 15-oz. can of whole peeled tomatoes, diced
> 1/2 lb. shredded sharp cheddar cheese
> 1 large onion diced
> 1/2 green bell pepper, diced
> 2 small cans of mushrooms
> 1 medium can of corn
> 1 15-oz. can of chili beans
> 8 oz. tomato sauce or spaghetti sauce
> 1 to 2 tbsp. of chili powder
> 1 tsp. garlic powder
> 1 tbsp. vinegar
> 1 tbsp. soy sauce
> 1 tsp. black pepper
> hot sauce or hot peppers to taste
> (Prepared as is, the chili will be mild.)

Instructions:

In a sauce pan, brown meat and lightly sauté onions. Add all other ingredients, except cheese, and simmer for 15 minutes. Stir in cheese and simmer for 5 more minutes. Makes 8 servings.

El Camino Real Vegetable Chowder

Ingredients:

1 cup kidney beans
1-1/2 cup lentils
1 pint stewed tomatoes
1 onion, chopped
1 green pepper, chopped
1 tomato, diced
2 potatoes, peeled and cut into 1/2 inch chunks
1/2 head of cauliflower, chopped
1 can corn
1/2 head of cabbage, chopped
2 tbsp. Worcestershire sauce
1/2 tsp. salt
1 tbsp. sugar
2 tsp. vinegar
2 bay leaves
1 tsp. chili powder

Instructions:

Cook beans for 1 hour. Drain. Fill pan 2/3 full of water and add all other ingredients. Simmer for 1 hour. Enjoy.

Big Tomato Vegetable Soup

Ingredients:

3/4 lb. ground beef
2 medium tomatoes, chopped
1 15-oz. can stewed tomatoes, chopped
1 7.5-oz.can tomato sauce
2 cups water
1 can red kidney beans
2 medium potatoes, diced
1 cup frozen corn niblets
2 cups cabbage, diced
2 stalks of celery, diced
1 large onion, diced
1-1/2 tsp. chili powder
1 tsp. oregano
1/2 tsp. garlic powder
1/2 cup cheddar cheese, grated
1/4 cup sour cream

Instructions:

In a medium sauce pan, brown ground beef, draining fat as you go. Add all other ingredients, and mix well. Bring to boil, simmer covered for 25 minutes. Serve sprinkled with grated cheese and dollop of sour cream. Serves 6.

Maxmilliano's Tortilla Soup

Ingredients:

1 14.5-oz. can tomatoes, diced
1/2 cup chopped green bell pepper
1/2 cup chopped onion
2 whole chicken breast, skinned and boned
2 cups water
1 14.5-oz. can beef broth
1 14.5-oz. can chicken broth

1 8.75-oz. can whole-kernel corn, drained
1 tsp. chili powder
1/2 tsp. ground cumin
3 cups tortilla chips, coarsely crushed
1 cup monterey jack cheese, shredded
1 avocado, peeled, seeded, and cut into chunks

Instructions:

Cut chicken into small cubes; set aside. In large saucepan, combine water, beef and chicken broth, tomatoes, onions and green peppers. Bring to boil. Add chicken, reduce heat. Cover and simmer for 10 minutes. Add corn, chili powder, cumin and pepper. Cover and simmer, for 10 minutes.

To serve, place crushed tortilla chips in bowl. Pour soup over chips. Sprinkle with cheese, avocado and cilantro. For an added touch, serve with lime wedges. Makes 6 servings.

Six Jalapeno Chili

Ingredients:

6 whole jalapeno peppers
2 lbs. ground beef
1 lb. rib eye steak (cut into 1/2 inch cubes)
1 tbsp Chili Powder
1/2 tsp Cayenne Pepper
1/2 Tbsp Cumin
1/2 Tbsp Oregano
4 cloves Garlic (minced)
1 tbsp Paprika
1/2 tbsp. Black Pepper
1-1/2 Tbsp lemon juice
1/2 cup Celery (sliced)
1/2 tbsp Basil
1/2 Green Pepper (chopped)
2 tbsp vinegar
Salt to taste (usually about 1/2 tsp)
Cornmeal (for thickening)

Instructions:

Boil jalapeno peppers in 3-4 cups water until soft; remove skins. Chop. (Save the liquid). In large skillet, brown meat; then add water until 2 inches over meat. Boil for 30 minutes. Add all other ingredients except cornmeal and simmer for 2 hours. Thicken the chili by adding 1-1/2 tbsp. cornmeal (more or less depending upon how thick you like it). If you like your chili fairly hot, add the reserved liquid from the peppers.

Fantastica Taco Soup

Ingredients:

1-1/2 lbs. ground chuck
1 onion, chopped
1 28-oz. can tomatoes
1 15-oz. can tomato sauce
2 10.5-oz. cans of cream of potato soup
1 10.5-oz. can beef broth
2 16-oz. cans kidney beans
1 1.25-oz. pkg. taco seasoning mix
crushed tortilla corn chips
1/2 lb. shredded cheddar cheese

Instructions:

Brown meat and onions in a deep skillet or Dutch oven. Drain grease. Add all remaining ingredients, except cheese and chips and simmer for 30-60 minutes. To serve, place crushed chips in individual bowls and pour soup over the chips. Garnish with cheese.

Jalapeño - Well known variety used fresh or pickled in many zesty Mexican Dishes. Has a medium hot flavor.

Not-so-wild Venison Chili

Ingredients:

2 tbsp. oil
1 lb. venison steak, cubed*
1 small onion, grated
1 small garlic bud, grated
3 tbsp. chili powder
1/2 tsp. oregano
1/4 to 1-1/2 tsp. cayenne pepper, depending on taste
3 cups hot water
1 tsp. salt

*You can substitute nearly any other meat if you like.

Instructions:

Place oil and meat in large skillet or Dutch oven and fry until brown. Add onion and garlic and sauté lightly. When onions are transparent, add salt, pepper, chili powder and oregano. Stir and add hot water. Cover and simmer 45 minutes (or until meat is tender). Add more water if needed. Makes 6 to 8 servings

Black Bean Chili

Ingredients

1 tbsp. vegetable oil
1-1/2 lbs. boneless round steak, cut into 3/4-inch pieces
1 large onion, chopped
2 cloves garlic, minced
2 14-oz. cans stewed tomatoes
1 14-oz. can chicken broth
1 6-oz. can tomato paste
2 4-oz. cans chopped green chilies
1 packet chili seasoning mix
3 16-oz. cans black beans, drained and rinsed
6 cups cooked rice
sour cream
fresh chopped cilantro

Instructions:

Heat oil in a large sauce pan over medium-high heat until hot. Add
steak and cook until steak is browned. Add onion and garlic. Cook
and stir 5 to 7 minutes or until onion is tender. Add tomatoes,
broth, tomato paste, chilies and seasoning mix. Bring to a boil.
Reduce heat, cover and simmer 20 to 30 minutes, stirring occasionally. Add beans. Cover and simmer 10 minutes more. Serve over
rice, garnish with sour cream and cilantro. Makes 6 servings.

Main Dishes

Fried Red Tomatoes

Ingredients:

4 to 6 tomatoes*
1/2 cup all-purpose flour
1/8 tsp. chili powder
2 tbsp. butter
2 tbsp. brown sugar
3/4 cup half-and-half
salt and pepper generously to taste
(1/2 tsp. of each is recommended)
salad herb seasoning

Instructions :

Cut the tomatoes into 3/4 -inch-thick slices. Mix together salt and pepper, flour and chile powder. Cover both side of tomatoes in flour, coating well and shaking off excess. Heat butter until foamy, but not browned. Cook tomatoes gently until first side is lightly browned. Before turning, crumble 1 tbsp. of brown sugar over the tops. Turn. Add extra butter if needed. Sprinkle remaining sugar over the tomatoes. Fry second sides until lightly browned. Remove tomatoes. Pour in half-and-half, stirring constantly, until thick and bubbly, then pour over tomatoes. Sprinkle with herb seasoning and serve. Makes 4-6 servings

*Green tomatoes can also be used.

Tender Tomato Stew

Ingredients:

2 small cans tomato sauce
1 chopped green pepper
4 medium-sized potatoes, cubed
6 carrots
1 cup celery
1 medium chopped onion
1 cup water
2 lbs. round steak, cut into 1 inch cubes
1-1/2 tsp. salt
1/4 tsp. pepper

Instructions:

Combine all ingredients, cover and cook for 5 hours at 250 degrees.

Jersey Rutgers - A classic variety named after one of the most tomato growing states.

Enchiladas Gringos

1 tbsp. vegetable oil
1 medium tomato, chopped
1/2 green pepper, chopped
1 small onion, chopped
2 cloves garlic, peeled and diced
1 large baked potato, peeled and cubed
1 cup pre-cooked roast beef or pork
2 cups enchilada sauce
12 corn tortillas
1 cup grated cheddar or colby jack cheese
4 green onions, thinly sliced
sour cream for serving

Preheat oven to 425 degrees. In a large skillet, heat oil and add the onion. Cook until soft. Add chopped meat, garlic, pepper, tomato and cubed potato. Cook about 3 minutes until warm through and starting to brown. Add about 1/2 cup of enchilada sauce, salt and pepper to taste. Simmer about 3 more minutes.

In a medium skillet, warm about 1 cup of the enchilada sauce. Remove from heat and dip each corn tortilla in the sauce, turning to coat both sides. Place tortilla in 9 x 14 inch baking dish and top with 1/3 cup of the filling. Roll up enchilada and push to end of dish. Continue process until all tortillas are filled, rolled and placed in the baking dish. Pour remaining sauce over enchiladas. Sprinkle cheese on top and bake about 15 minutes or until heated and bubbling. Sprinkle green onions over top and serve with sour cream.

44 Chili & Tomato Macaroni

Ingredients:

1-1/2 lbs. ground beef chuck
2-1/4 peeled fresh tomatoes (may substitute No. 2 can)
1 chopped bell pepper
1/2 chopped onion
1/2 cup mushrooms
2 tbsp. butter
1 cup water
8 oz. macaroni, cooked
1/2 tsp. Tabasco sauce
1/4 tsp. salt

Instructions:

In heavy skillet, cook meat, onion and butter, stirring frequently until brown. Add water, peppers, mushrooms, and salt; cover and simmer for 20 minutes, then add tomatoes, Tabasco sauce, and drained, cooked macaroni. Continue simmering for 20 minutes. Enjoy! Serves 5.

Yankee Taco

Ingredients:

   1 lb. sirloin tip steak
   1 jalapeno pepper, chopped
   1 bell pepper chopped
   1/2 cup mushrooms
   1 medium-sized onion, diced
   3 medium-sized potatoes
   1/2 lb. grated mild American cheese
   1 pkg. flour tortillas
   1 tbsp. Tabasco sauce
   salsa
   sour cream

Instructions:

Peel and cut potatoes into 1/2 inch cubes; boil. Cut sirloin tips
into pieces approx. 1/2 inch square. Fry in small amount of oil until
cooked through. Add peppers, onion, mushrooms, and Tabasco to
meat. Add potatoes just prior to serving. Spoon mixture onto
tortilla. Cover with cheese and fold over. Cover with salsa and a
spoonful of sour cream.

Pondering Peppers

-The degree of "heat" in a pepper is measured in Scoville heat units, named for Wilbur Scoville, the pharmacist who developed the heat grading system.

-Each variety of pepper is different in its flavor, and heat. The hottest pepper currently known, the Mexican Habanero, produces 350,000 Scoville heat units. By contrast, the Cayenne pepper generates only 20,000 units.

-The chemical that makes peppers hot, Capaicin, is tasteless and odorless. The flavor one enjoys from the pepper comes from other chemicals inside the pepper walls and seeds.

Habanero - Very hot. 100 times
hotter than Jalapeno varieties.
Has a savory aftertaste.

Spaghetti Mexico Style

Ingredients:

1 qt. stewed tomatoes
1 can tomato sauce
1 tbsp. vinegar
1 lb. ground beef
1 16-oz. can corn
1 tbsp. salt
1 chopped large bell pepper
2 small jalapeno peppers, chopped
1 tbsp. Tabasco sauce
1 large minced onion
1 tsp. Worcestershire sauce
1 tsp. chili powder
1/2 lb. mozzarella cheese, grated
1/2 lb. spaghetti noodles.

Instructions:

Brown ground beef in saucepan. Drain grease. In separate pan, pour stewed tomatoes, tomato sauce, peppers, onions, corn, vinegar, Tabasco sauce, chili powder, Worcestershire sauce and salt. Bring mixture to boil stirring regularly. Add hamburger. Simmer slowly for 15-25 minutes while spaghetti noodles are boiling in separate pan. When noodles are ready, serve by placing on plate and pouring sauce on top, then adding grated cheese.

Chubby Enchiladas

Ingredients:

    1 lb. ground chuck*
    1 onion, chopped
    1 clove garlic, minced
    1/2 cup grated cheddar cheese
    1 tablespoon oil
    2 cups basic red enchilada sauce
    12 corn tortillas
    salt to taste

Instructions:

To make filling, sauté onion and garlic in oil until onion is transparent; add meat and brown. Season with salt to taste. Add enchilada sauce and cheese and simmer for 10 minutes. In separate, oiled pan, fry tortillas. Drain and then immerse tortillas in hot sauce. Spread the filling across the tortilla and roll tightly. Pour remaining sauce on top and add shredded cheese. Put under broiler or heat at 350 degrees until cheese melts. Serves 4.

*For chicken enchiladas, substitute 3 cups of shredded cooked chicken for the ground chuck.

Frijoles Chards

Ingredients:

5 jalapeno peppers, stemmed, seeded and diced
1/2 green pepper, chopped
4 medium sized tomatoes, diced
1 lb. dried pinto beans
2 large onions, chopped
6 garlic cloves, minced
6 bacon strips, chopped
1/2 cup ham, chopped, and thinly sliced
1/2 cup cilantro leaves chopped
4 green onions, chopped
1/2 chicken bouillon cube
salt to taste.

Instructions:

Thoroughly rinse beans under hot water. Place beans in large
saucepan and add water, bacon, peppers, chopped onions, jalapenos,
tomatoes, ham, and garlic. Bring to a boil, cover and reduce heat.
Simmer on low heat for about 1-1/2 hours until beans are soft. Stir
in green onions, chopped cilantro, bouillon cube, and salt. Simmer
for 30-minutes more. Serves 6.

La Raza Corn Casserole

Ingredients:

2 cups tomato sauce or puree
1 tbsp. olive oil
1 onion, minced
1/2 green chile, diced
3 cups corn (fresh, frozen or canned)
2 tbsp. butter or margarine
1/4 lb. grated cheese
salt and pepper to taste

Instructions:

In large saucepan, sauté onion in hot oil until cooked through.
Add remaining ingredients. Mix well. Pour into a buttered casserole
dish and bake at 350 degrees for 1 hour. Remove from oven and
sprinkle cheese on top.
Serves 6.

Broiled Tomatoes with Feta Cheese

Ingredients:

   3 large tomatoes sliced about 1/2" thick
   4 oz. feta cheese
   1/2 tbsp. marjoram, chopped
   olive oil
   black pepper

Instructions:

Preheat broiler. Place tomatoes in the bottom of a large lightly oiled baking pan. Crumble cheese over tomatoes. Sprinkle half the marjoram on top of cheese. Broil until cheese is melted. Remove, sprinkle with a little more oil on top and the rest of the marjoram. Season with pepper to taste and serve. Makes 4 servings.

Red October - Classic tomato named for its ability to remain on the vine longer than other varieties. Keeps longer after harvest too.

Italian Noodles & Beef

Ingredients:

1 lb. ground beef
1/4 green pepper, chopped
1 large onion, chopped
1 8-oz. can mushrooms
1/4 tsp. oregano
1 cup tomato soup
1 16-oz. can tomato paste
1/4 cup water
1 tbsp. Worcestershire sauce
4 oz. elbow noodles, cooked and drained
1/2 lb. sharp, cheddar cheese, grated
salt and pepper to taste

Instructions:

Brown ground beef. Add green pepper, onion, mushrooms and oregano. Sauté until all vegetables are tender. Add water, tomato soup, tomato paste, Worcestershire sauce, salt and pepper.

Grease casserole dish and layer noodles, meat sauce, and cheese; repeat process until all ingredients are used. Bake at 375 degrees for 45 minutes. Serves 6.

The Chili & Tomato Burger

Ingredients:

1-1/2 lbs. ground beef
1/2 cup diced monterey jack cheese (2 oz.)
1/2 tsp. pepper
1/4 tsp. salt
1 4-oz. can chopped green chilies, drained
1 large tomato, diced.

Instructions:

Preheat oven broiler. In a large bowl, knead all ingredients into ball. Then, flatten into 6 patties. Place patties on rack in broiler pan. Broil with tops 3 to 4 inches from heat until cooked through. (Turn once.) Place patties on bun with spreads and garnishes the way you like them. Serves 6.

Renaissance Rice

Ingredients:

3/4 cup uncooked rice
2 tbsp. olive oil or shortening
3/4 lb. lean ground beef
1/2 bell pepper, chopped
1 medium onion, chopped
1/3 cup celery, chopped
1 can (2 cups) stewed tomatoes
1/2 cup water
2 tsp. sugar
1-1/2 tsp. salt
1/2 tsp. black pepper

Instructions:

Boil rice according to directions on package. Heat oil in skillet.
Add ground beef, rice, and onion; simmer, stirring frequently until
rice and meat are brown and onion is soft. Add pepper and celery.
Cook for 5 minutes on low heat, stirring frequently. Add remaining
ingredients; cover and simmer for 30 minutes stirring occasionally.
Serves 6

Tomato Chili Rice

Ingredients:

1 medium tomato, diced
2 cups cooked rice
1/2 can cream of celery soup
1/2 pint sour cream
1/2 lb. grated American cheese
1 can diced green chili
salt and pepper to taste

Instructions:

Mix all ingredients. Bake in buttered pan at 350 for 30 minutes or until bubbling.

Hot Lemon - A variety hailing from South America, this pepper has a unique citrus echo in its savory taste. Moderately hot.

Southwestern Italian Sausage

Ingredients:

1 lb. franks (8 to 10)
2 tbsp. butter or margarine
1 can tomato soup
1/4 cup brown sugar
1/4 cup water
3 tbsp. vinegar
1 tbsp. Worcestershire sauce
1/2 lemon, thinly sliced
1/4 cup chopped green pepper
jalapeno peppers, chopped (according to taste)
1 medium tomato, chopped

Instructions:

Cut franks in thirds. Butter skillet and lightly brown franks. Add all ingredients to skillet except peppers and tomatoes. Cover and simmer for 10 minutes. Add peppers and tomatoes and simmer covered for an additional 10 minutes. Serve alone or over hot pasta or rice.

Sonoran Style Spanish Rice

Ingredients:

1-1/2 cups rice
3 cups water
3 tbsp. shortening or oil
1 cup canned tomatoes
2 medium fresh tomatoes, chopped
1/2 cup bell pepper, chopped
1/2 cup red bell pepper, chopped
1 jalapeno peppers, chopped
1 medium garlic clove, crushed
1/2 cup onion, chopped
1/4 tsp. cumin
1-1/2 tsp. salt
pepper to taste

Instructions:

Melt shortening in large skillet. Add rice and cook on medium heat until rice is golden-brown. Reduce heat and add onion, peppers, tomatoes, garlic, salt, black pepper and cumin. Mix well and add enough water to cover the rice, (about 1-1/2 cups). Cover and let simmer until almost dry. While still cooking over low heat, add remaining water, a little at a time; cook until fluffy. Serves 6.

Pepper Potatoes

Ingredients:

3 medium potatoes, peeled and cut into 1/4 inch slices
2 red bell peppers, sliced into 1/4 inch rings
2 medium onions, cut into 1/4 inch slices
1/4 lb. baked or smoked ham cut into small chunks
3 tbsp. olive oil
1/4 cup parsley
1 garlic clove, minced
1/2 lb. American cheese, grated
salt and pepper to taste

Instructions:

Preheat oven to 375 degrees. In a large mixing bowl, combine potatoes, peppers, onions, ham, garlic, salt and pepper. Pour olive oil over mixture and mix until coated. Oil or spray with non-stick spray coating a 13" x 9" pan. Place mixture in baking dish, cover with foil and bake for 45 minutes or until vegetables are tender. Remove from oven and sprinkle with cheese and parsley. Let stand until cheese has melted.

Donja Maria's Chile Relleno En Casserole

Ingredients:

- 1 lb. lean ground beef
- 1 medium tomato, chopped
- 1-1/2 cups sharp cheddar cheese
- 1/2 cup chopped onion
- 1-1/2 cups milk
- vegetable oil
- 1/4 cup flour
- 4 eggs beaten
- 2 4-oz. cans whole green chilies, seeded & halved crosswise
- 1/2 tsp. salt
- 1/4 tsp. pepper

Instructions:

In skillet, brown beef, onion, salt, and pepper in a little oil; drain off excess fat. Place half the chilies in a greased 10" x 6" x 1-1/2" casserole dish, sprinkle with cheese. Add meat mixture and another layer of chilies. Combine remaining ingredients and beat until smooth. Pour over meat mixture and bake for 45 minutes (until knife comes out clean) at 350 degrees. Allow to cool for about five minutes, and cut into 8 squares. Makes 8 servings.

Corn-Stuffed Baja Tomatoes

Ingredients:

8 medium tomatoes
1 chopped green pepper
2 10-oz. packages frozen kernel corn
1/4 cup minced onion
2 tbsp. vegetable oil
1 tsp. thyme
1 tsp. basil
pepper to taste
1/4 cup bread crumbs
1/2 lb. grated mozzarella cheese
2 tbsp. butter or margarine, melted

Instructions:

Preheat oven to 400 degrees. Cut the tops off tomatoes and scoop out seeds and pulp, leaving enough pulp to keep the tomato skin intact. Place tomatoes upside down on plate or paper towel and drain. Heat corn in sauce pan. In separate skillet, sauté onion and green pepper in oil until onion is transparent. Add corn, thyme and basil. Season to taste with pepper. Stir on low heat for 2-5 minutes more. Fill tomatoes with corn mixture. Place tomatoes in shallow baking dish and sprinkle tops with crumbs. Place 1/4 pat of margarine and cheese atop each tomato. Bake 10 to 15 minutes or until heated through. Serves 4

Mushroom-Pepper Chicken

Ingredients:

1-1/2 lbs. boneless, skinless chicken
1 large onion, chopped
1 can cream of chicken soup
1 can cream of mushroom soup
1 can stewed tomatoes
1 cup sour cream
1 small can chopped green chilies
1 (10-count) package corn tortillas
2 cups cheddar cheese, grated
1 small can black olives, sliced

Instructions:

Cut chicken meat into small pieces. Add onions and stir fry. In separate large bowl, mix soups, tomatoes, sour cream and chopped chilies; set this mixture aside. Cut tortillas into strips 1/2 inch wide. Grease a 9x13-inch pan and place a layer of corn tortillas on the bottom. Add a layer of chicken and then a layer of sauce. Repeat until all materials are used up. Sprinkle cheese and sliced black olives on top. Bake at 350 degrees for 25 minutes.
Serves 6.

More Pondering Peppers

-Capaicin, the chemical which makes chili peppers hot, has many other uses. It is an important component in pepper spray used by policemen, liniment rubs for rheumatism, and throat lozenges, just to name a few.

-Capaicin can still be detected by humans when diluted 17 million times.

-Capaicin is a powerful and stable alkaloid. It is somewhat soluble in water, but very soluble in fats and oils. That's why it stays with a person after eating.

Jalapa - A variation on the Jalapeno, this pepper has a slightly more mild flavor than its relative.

Sicilian Tomatoes & Mozzarella

Ingredients:

4 medium tomatoes, sliced
8 cups soft bread cubes
3 cups shredded mozzarella cheese
4 bacon strips, crispy cooked and crumbled
1/2 cup butter or margarine, melted
1/2 cup chopped celery
1/2 cup chopped onion
2 eggs, beaten
1/2 tsp. garlic salt
1/2 tsp. dried oregano

Instructions:

Place a single layer of tomatoes (about half of what you have) in a greased 13x9x2-inch baking dish; set aside. In a large bowl, combine bread cubes, 2 cups of cheese, bacon, butter, celery, onion, eggs, garlic salt and oregano; mix well. Spoon mixture over tomatoes. Top with remaining tomatoes and sprinkle with cheese. Bake, uncovered, at 350° for 30 minutes or until heated through. Serves 6.

Spaghetti in a Skillet

Ingredients:

1 lb. ground beef
1 16-oz. can tomato paste
1 18-oz. can tomato juice
3 cups cold water
1-1/2 tsp. chili powder
1 tsp. garlic salt
1 tsp. sugar
1 tsp. oregano
2 tbsp. instant onion
1 7-oz. pkg. spaghetti noodles (uncooked)
salt to taste

Instructions:

Brown ground beef in skillet and pour off excess grease. Add all
remaining ingredients except spaghetti to meat. Cover and simmer
for 35 minutes. Add spaghetti, stirring it in as it softens. Cover
and simmer for another 30 minutes or until spaghetti is tender,
stirring frequently. Garnish with Parmesan cheese. Serves 4 to 6.

Alberto's Green Chili Stew

Ingredients:

1/2 cup green chile, peeled and chopped
1-1/2 lbs. cubed beef stew meat
1 15-oz can corn or equivalent frozen package
1 15-oz. can kidney beans
1 medium onion, chopped
2 potatoes, peeled and cubed
2 cans chopped stewed tomatoes
2 cloves garlic, finely chopped
salt and pepper to taste

Instructions:

Sauté meat with onions until brown. Drain. Add chile, beans, corn, and potatoes. Add water until everything in pan is covered and simmer for about 1 hour or until meat is tender. Add potatoes and additional water as needed. Add all other ingredients and simmer for 10 minutes more. Keep adding water as needed so stew gravy is the consistency you like.

Leprechaun Chicken Enchiladas

Ingredients:

12 to 18 corn tortillas
1/2 cup oil
8 oz. shredded monterey jack cheese
3/4 cup chopped onion
1/4 cup butter or margarine
1/4 cup flour
2 cups chicken broth
4 oz. chopped green chilies
1 cup sour cream
1 chicken or 3 breast halves, boiled and shredded

Instructions:

Very briefly plunge tortillas in hot oil until softened (for about 5 seconds). Place some chicken, cheese, and onion on each tortilla and roll up. Place seam side down in greased baking pan. In a separate sauce pan, over low heat, melt butter. Add flour and broth; cook till thick. Stir in sour cream and chilies. Pour over enchiladas. Bake at 375 degrees for 20 minutes or until everything is heated through. Spread remaining cheese on top and return to oven for 5 more minutes. Garnish with chopped green onions and a sprig of fresh cilantro. Serves 6.

Vegetarian Stuffed Tomatoes

Ingredients:

8 medium-sized tomatoes
1/4 lb. long-grain rice
1 large onion, chopped
1 large green bell pepper, chopped
2 tbsp. butter
1 tsp. salt
1/4 tsp. pepper
1/4 tsp. season salt of choice
grated Parmesan cheese

Instructions:

Put rice on to boil according to directions on package. Slice tomatoes in half and scoop out centers being careful to leave pulp on the sides. Sauté onion and green pepper in butter. Drain water from rice and add salt, pepper, and season salt. Stuff tomatoes with rice mixture, sprinkle Parmesan cheese on top, and bake at 350° for 30 minutes. Serves 8.

Sweet Tangerine - Once you see one of these tomatoes you will understand where it's name came from. Very sweet variety with a distinctive orange color.

3-Chili Stew

Ingredients:

1-1/2 lbs. beef, cubed
1 tbsp. vegetable oil
1 cup hot water
3 4-oz. cans chopped green chilies
1/2 red pepper, chopped
1 jalapeno pepper, chopped
1 tbsp. beef granules
3 medium potatoes, peeled and cubed
2 medium onions, chopped
1 8-oz. can stewed tomatoes
3 medium carrots, peeled and sliced
2 tbsp. Tabasco sauce
1 clove garlic, minced
1 tsp. salt
1/4 tsp. cumin

Instructions:

Pour vegetable oil into heavy pot or Dutch oven. Brown meat in oil. Mix beef granules in 1 cup of water; add to pot. Cover pot and cook until meat is tender. Add all other ingredients and simmer for 35 to 40 minutes. Garnish with fresh chopped, cilantro and serve. Feeds 6.

Easy Manicotti

Ingredients:

1 lb. ground beef
1/2 large onion, chopped
1/2 lb. mozzarella cheese, grated
1 small container of cottage cheese
1/2 cup mayonnaise
1 1/2 pkg. manicotti noodles
medium jar ragu sauce

Instructions:

Cook noodles as directed. In medium skillet, sauté meat and onion until meat is brown and onion is clear. Remove from heat, pour off grease. Stir in cottage cheese, mayonnaise and Mozzarella cheese. Pour water from noodles. Stuff noodles with mixture. Pour Ragu sauce over mixture and bake for 30 minutes at 350 degrees.

Viva Italia - A very sweet variety related to the Roma family. Great for sauces and salsas because it has a high solid flesh content.

Salsa & Appetizers

3-Alarm Salsa

Ingredients:

  2 qts. stewed tomatoes
  1 large green pepper chopped
  3 jalapeno peppers chopped
  1 large onion chopped
  1 tbsp. vinegar
  1 tsp. sugar
  Tabasco sauce to taste

Instructions:

Combine all ingredients except Tabasco sauce in a pan and bring to a slow boil. Simmer for 45 minutes. Pour into small bowls and serve with corn tortilla chips for dipping.

Serving tip #1: Into each bowl add grated American cheese to the top or sprinkle grated cheese on top of tortilla chips and melt in microwave.

Serving tip #2: Since different people enjoy different levels of heat, add Tabasco sauce in varying amounts to various bowls as you serve. For those who don't like it very hot, add none - if they really like it hot, add 2 tbsp.

20 Gringos Salsa Fresca

Ingredients:

4 ripe roma tomatoes*
3 serrano chilies, minced
1 clove garlic, minced
1/2 small onion, chopped
1/2 bell pepper, chopped
1 tbsp. oil
1/2 tsp. salt
1 tbsp. cider vinegar or freshly squeezed lime juice

*Use only fresh roma tomatoes.

Instructions:

Put tomatoes into boiling water to loosen skins. Remove from hot water and run cold water over tomatoes to cool. Core tomatoes and remove skins, then roughly dice. For less heat, remove seeds from Serrano's before mincing. Put all ingredients into blender and process briefly. Let stand in refrigerator 1/2 hour before serving. Makes 1 1/2 cups. For slightly different flavor, substitute jalapeno peppers for serranos.

Salsa Acapulco

Ingredients:

1 28-oz. can stewed tomatoes
3 large jalapenos
4 large garlic cloves peeled
1/2 tsp. cumin powder
1/2 tsp. oregano
1/4 cup cilantro leaves
1 tbsp. lemon juice
1/4 tsp. salt

Instructions:

Roast jalapenos (in the oven under broiler) until skins are blackened. Do not remove seeds or skins, but remove stems. Blend jalapenos, seasonings, garlic, and juice of tomatoes, (do not add tomatoes at this point, only their juice). When fully blended, add tomatoes, lemon juice, and cilantro leaves, and chop in blender for 3 seconds. Refrigerate for 30 minutes before serving.

Salsa Baja California

Ingredients:

2 cloves garlic, peeled and chopped
2 lbs. (about 4 large) tomatoes, broiled
5 serrano chilies, broiled
2 tbsp. safflower oil
1/2 medium onion, finely chopped
1/2 tsp. salt

Instructions:

Place the tomatoes, garlic, and chilies into blender and blend to a
slightly textured sauce. Set aside. In a separate frying pan, heat oil;
add onion and salt; cook gently until translucent—about 3 minutes.
Add blended ingredients and cook on high heat, stirring regularly
for 7 to 8 minutes, until slightly reduced and thickened. There
should be flecks of brown in the sauce.

Tomatillo Salsa Verde

Ingredients:

- 10 tomatillos
- 2 jalapeno peppers
- 1/4 cup chopped cilantro
- 1/2 small white onion
- salt to taste

Instructions:

Remove husks of tomatillos and wash under water. Boil tomatillos for 10 minutes. Meanwhile, roast jalapenos over burner until black all around. Remove blackened skin with a paper towel or dry cloth. Remove seeds and chop. Chop onion. Add tomatillos, jalapenos, cilantro and onion. Blend until smooth. Add salt to taste. Refrigerate for 30 minutes before serving.

Jalapeno - One of the most widely used and widely available of the hot peppers. Moderately hot. Great for Mexican dishes.

Old Santa Fe Salsa Fresca

Ingredients:

4 chopped tomatoes
4 green bell peppers, chopped
*4 jalapeno chilies, chopped
1 medium red onion, chopped
1 clove garlic, minced
2 tbsp. cilantro, minced
2 tbsp. vegetable oil
2 tbsp. fresh lime juice
1 tsp. ground cumin
1/4 tsp. ground cloves

*According to taste

Instructions:

Thoroughly mix all ingredients. Refrigerate for at least 1 hour before serving.

Backyard Grill Salsa

Ingredients:

10 medium tomatoes (roma are best)
1 large onion
2 jalapeno peppers
3 anaheim peppers
4 tbsp. olive oil
1 small can spicy V8 juice
4 tbsp. lime juice
3 cilantro leaves, chopped.
1 tsp. salt

Instructions:

Quarter tomatoes and onions and place all vegetables in a bowl.
Add olive oil and salt. Stir, making sure flavor covers all vegetables.
Empty bowl of vegetable mixture onto medium- hot grill. Use care
to avoid burning the peppers. Cook vegetables until onions are
cooked through and the tomato skins are ready to lift off. Remove
all vegetables and peel tomatoes. Place vegetable mixture into
blender or food processor. Add V8, lime juice, and cilantro. Blend or
chop to desired salsa texture.

78 Ensenada Style Black Bean Salsa

Ingredients:

1 bell pepper, chopped,
jalapeno pepper, roasted, peeled, stemmed, seeded, & diced.
2 cups black beans, cooked and drained
2 tbsp. pomegranate, or cranberry juice
1/4 cup yellow bell pepper, chopped
1/4 cup red bell pepper, chopped
3 roasted garlic cloves, chopped
1 medium onion, chopped
1 tbsp. chilies chipotle (canned)
1 tbsp. fresh chopped cilantro
salt to taste
1/4 lb grated cheddar cheese

Instructions:

Combine all ingredients except cheese in medium saucepan. Toss briefly over medium heat. Pour into glass serving bowls and serve. Sprinkle cheese over top and enjoy with tortilla chips. Makes 4 cups.

Maria's Guacamole Especial

Ingredients:

- 3 large avocados, peeled, pitted, and mashed
- 1 tomato, chopped
- 3 tbsp., chopped onion
- 2 garlic cloves, mashed
- 1 tsp. olive oil
- 3 tbsp. lime juice
- 1/2 tsp. salt

Instructions:

Thoroughly blend all ingredients in a bowl. Serve with chips, or as a garnish or side dish.

Serrano Chili - A very common pepper. Moderately hot with a mild, easy to use flavor.

Quick & Easy Salsa

Ingredients:

2-3/4 lbs tomatoes, peeled and chopped
(approximately 5 medium-sized tomatoes)
1 14-oz. can tomato sauce
3 jalapeno peppers, chopped
3 serrano peppers, chopped
3 sprigs cilantro
1 carrot, minced
3 cloves garlic, minced
1-1/2 tsp. lemon or lime juice
1 tsp. salt

Instructions:

Combine and mix all ingredients in large bowl. Refrigerate for half
an hour before serving for best results. Makes 2 quarts salsa.

Mama's Favorite Pico De Gallo

Ingredients:

3 medium tomatoes, diced
3 large spanish onions, chopped
2 medium avocados, peeled, pitted, and diced
3 leaves fresh cilantro, chopped fine
1 tsp. lemon juice
jalapenos, chopped, to taste (2 for mild, 8 for hot)

Instructions:

Mix all ingredients together. Refrigerate for 1 to 2 hours. Serve as dip, with fajitas or as a side dish or garnish.

"To Die For" Salsa Picante

Ingredients:

16 large tomatoes, chopped
2 red chilies, chopped
2 green chilies, chopped
4 large, white onions, chopped
2 jalapeno peppers, chopped
1 serrano pepper, chopped
1 cup white vinegar
1/2 tsp. celery salt
1 tsp. garlic, crushed
1/2 tsp. mustard seed
1/2 lb. cheddar cheese, grated

Instructions:

Place all ingredients into large skillet and simmer over low heat for 2 hours. Pour into serving bowls and sprinkle cheese on top. Makes 3 quarts.

All-Purpose Red Chili Sauce

Ingredients:

1 cup tomato juice
2 tbsp. shortening
3/4 tsp. salt
2 tbsp. flour
1/2 tsp. garlic salt
1/2 cup red chile powder
1/2 tsp. oregano
1 cup cold water

Instructions:

Melt shortening in saucepan on medium heat. Stir in flour and cook for 1 minute. Add chile powder and cook for an additional minute. Gradually add tomato juice and water and stir constantly; don't allow lumps to form. Add remaining ingredients and simmer at low heat for 10-15 minutes. Makes one pint.

Yellow Cayenne - A sweeter tasting cayenne variety, this moderately hot pepper may be used well in a number of recipes.

Salsa Tropica

Ingredients:

2/3 cup crushed pineapple
1/4 cup red bell peppers, diced
2 tsp. fresh lime juice
1 tsp. fresh lemon juice
1 jalapeno pepper, chopped with seeds and
    membranes removed
1 1/2 tbsp. fresh basil, finely chopped
1-1/2 tsp. red wine vinegar
1/2 tsp. sugar

Instructions:

Combine all ingredients in medium bowl and mix well. Refrigerate for 1 hour before serving. Serves 4.

Down-Town Salsa

Ingredients:

1-1/2 cups chopped green bell peppers
6 cups tomatoes, chopped with skins removed
3 large, white onions
3 garlic cloves, chopped
2 to 6 jalapeno peppers
   (depending upon how hot you like it)
1 tbsp. fresh lime
2 tbsp. white vinegar
1 15-oz. can tomato sauce
2 tbsp. salt
2 tbsp. fresh, chopped, cilantro (stems removed)
4 tbsp. cornstarch dissolved in 1/2 cup cold water

Instructions:

Put all vegetables into large skillet. Add tomato sauce, salt, vinegar, and lime juice. Simmer for 15 minutes. Stir in cornstarch and bring entire mixture to a boil. Makes 2 quarts.

Salsa Espanja

Ingredients:

3/4 cup tomatoes, chopped
1/3 cup onion, chopped
2 garlic cloves, minced
3 chopped jalapenos (or serranos for extra heat)
1 tbsp. minced cilantro
salt to taste
2 tbsp. lime juice

Instructions:

Mix ingredients in large bowl. Set aside at room temperature to season for about 30 minutes before serving.

Sun Gold - A very colorful variety of miniature tomato, the Sun Gold has a unique tangy flavor that is best enjoyed raw.

Salsa Fiesta

Ingredients:

2 medium tomatoes, chopped
1 4-oz. can chopped black olives
1 4-oz. can chopped green chilies
1/2 cup chopped onion
3 tbsp. green onions, chopped
1, 2, or 3 chopped jalapeno peppers to taste
3 tbsp. olive oil
1-1/2 tbsp. vinegar
1 tsp. garlic salt

Instructions:

Combine all ingredients into large bowl.
Refrigerate several hours before serving. Enjoy!

Four Pepper Party Dip

Ingredients:

1 serrano pepper, chopped
1 jalapeno pepper, chopped
1/2 green bell pepper, chopped
1/2 red bell pepper, chopped
8 oz. cream cheese, softened
1/8 tsp. lemon pepper
1 to 5 tbsp. mayonnaise
1/2 tsp. salt

Instructions:

Combine all peppers in a bowl. Add cream cheese and blend well. Add mayonnaise for taste and desired consistency. Blend in lemon pepper. Serve with crackers or tostada chips. Serves 8 to 10.

Smokin' Bean Dip

Ingredients:

1 16-oz. can refried beans
1 small onion, chopped
1 4-oz. can jalapeno peppers, chopped (drained)
1/4 lb. cheddar cheese, shredded
2 tbsp. butter or margarine
salt and pepper to taste

Instructions:

Sauté onions in butter or margarine until clear. Add all other ingredients and stir over low heat. Serve warm with grated cheddar cheese on top for dipping corn or tortilla chips. Serves 10.

Winter Red - Developed to be picked green and stored after harvest. The Winter Red has a low juice content and firm structure.

Recipe Notes:

Recipe Notes:

Recipe Notes:

Recipe Notes:

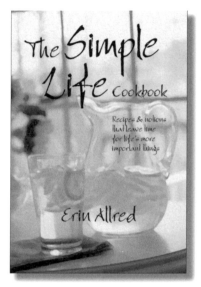

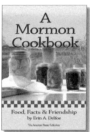